THE NO MONEY NIGHTMARE

WAKING UP TO THE REALITY OF GETTING OLDER...AND SECURING YOUR FINANCIAL FUTURE

NOAH WAYAN

TOP ARTISTS 4U LLC

First Printing, 2026

ISBN

Paperback - 13: 978-1-968871-77-2

Ebook - 13: 978-1-968871-78-9

Top Artists 4 U LLC

15021 Ventura Blvd. #783 Sherman Oaks, CA 91403

TopArtists4U@gmail.com

DISCLAIMER

This book reflects the author's personal experience and general observations about financial planning in later life. It is intended for informational and motivational purposes only and does not constitute professional financial, legal, or tax advice.

Every individual's financial situation is unique. Please consult a licensed financial advisor before making significant financial decisions.

INTRODUCTION

WHEN THE NUMBERS BECOME PERSONAL

There comes a point in life when financial conversations stop being theoretical and become personal. Retirement is no longer something you hear about from older relatives or read about in articles aimed at young professionals. It becomes your situation. Your numbers. Your timeline. Your responsibility.

For many people, this moment does not arrive with panic. It arrives quietly. You log into a retirement account and notice the balance is smaller than you expected. You check your projected Social Security benefit and realize it will not cover your current lifestyle. You consider how many working years you realistically have left and understand that time is no longer unlimited. Nothing dramatic may have happened, yet something feels unsettled. You sense that if no adjustments are made, the future may feel tighter than you imagined.

This book was written for that moment.

It is not a book about becoming wealthy overnight. It is not a book about extreme investing strategies or chasing unrealistic returns. It is not written for someone in their twenties with decades of compounding ahead. It is written for the individual between fifty-five and sixty-five who has worked hard, lived responsibly, and now recognizes that their financial foundation may not be strong enough to carry them comfortably into later life.

If you see yourself in that description, you are not alone. Many intelligent, capable adults arrive at this stage with less saved than they intended. Life rarely unfolds in perfect alignment with long-term projections. Income fluctuates. Family responsibilities increase. Health expenses arise. Opportunities appear and disappear. Years pass quickly while attention is focused on immediate demands. By the time retirement becomes a serious consideration, the gap between expectation and reality can feel uncomfortable.

The purpose of this book is not to shame you for the past. It is to stabilize your future.

You may not be able to rebuild decades of missed saving. You may not be able to retire exactly as you once imagined. But you are not without leverage. You still have earning capacity. You still have decision power. You still have time to restructure your life deliberately rather than drift into uncertainty.

Throughout these pages, you will face your numbers calmly. You will calculate your true expenses. You will identify your guaranteed income. You will measure your retirement gap. You will examine the levers you still control, including housing, income structure, expenses, benefit timing, and health. You will follow a clear twelve-month reset plan designed specifically for this stage of life. The goal is not luxury. The goal is sustainable stability.

Retirement, as presented in popular culture, often looks like a reward that automatically follows age. In reality, retirement is a financial equation. When the equation is unbalanced, the answer is not denial. The answer is adjustment. Adjustment requires clarity. Clarity requires courage. Courage begins with honest assessment.

If you have felt the quiet tightening that comes from realizing you may be behind, this book is your next step forward. It will not offer fantasy solutions, but it will offer structure. It will not promise effortless comfort, but it will show you how to reduce risk and regain control. It will guide you away from vague hope and toward deliberate design.

You are not too late to act. You are at a decision point. The direction you choose now can meaningfully influence the decades ahead. Stability is built intentionally, and intention begins here.

PART ONE

THE SLOW REALIZATION

ONE
THE MUSICIAN WHO THOUGHT THE GIGS WOULD NEVER STOP
AND THE PATTERN NO ONE PLANS FOR

There is a pattern that unfolds quietly in many lives, and it rarely begins with irresponsibility or neglect. It begins with work. Steady work. The kind that pays the bills, sustains a lifestyle, and builds confidence year after year. Income flows in. Expenses are covered. Adjustments are made during lean seasons. Good months compensate for slower ones. From the outside, everything appears stable. From the inside, there is no immediate reason to worry.

William's story is one version of that pattern.

For nearly three decades, he earned his living as a performing musician. He built a reputation as reliable, talented, and professional. He worked weddings, corporate events, clubs, private functions, and occasional touring support slots. He was never famous, but he was respected. His calendar stayed full enough that he rarely questioned where the next check would come from. Some months were heavy with bookings and others were thin, but over the course of a year the income usually balanced out well enough for him to live comfortably.

He did not consider himself wealthy, but he did not consider himself broke either. He paid his rent on time, upgraded his car every few years, invested in quality equipment, and allowed himself small luxuries when a season had been strong. From the outside, his life appeared stable. He worked consistently, maintained relationships in the industry, and adapted as trends shifted. What he did not build, however, was structure beneath his income.

As an independent earner, his money came in waves. During strong seasons he felt relaxed about finances. During slower stretches he tightened spending temporarily and waited for bookings to improve. Taxes were handled inconsistently. Some years he filed carefully and paid what he owed. Other years he minimized reported income to survive leaner periods, promising himself he would make up the difference later. Retirement planning always felt like something he would address once his schedule became more predictable. He heard about IRAs and long-term investing, but those conversations felt abstract compared to equipment repairs, travel expenses, and everyday living.

Time moved forward quietly. In his early forties, retirement seemed distant enough to ignore. In his late forties, he noticed small physical changes—slower recovery after long nights, more fatigue after back-to-back performances-but his bookings remained steady. In his early fifties, he heard peers discuss pensions and 401(k)s, yet he convinced himself musicians followed a different rhythm. Artists worked longer. Talent did not retire at sixty-five. He believed that if he ever needed to accelerate his savings, he could simply take on more gigs and increase his income quickly.

By his mid-fifties, subtle shifts began to surface. Younger performers entered the market with lower rates and stronger online branding. Clients occasionally asked whether he had "younger energy" available for certain events. Securing the same volume of work required more effort. When he reviewed his annual earnings over several years, he saw a gradual downward trend. It was not catastrophic, but it was consistent.

At fifty-eight, curiosity led him to log into the Social Security website. He assumed his benefit would provide a reasonable safety net. Instead, he found a projected monthly payment far lower than he expected. Years of inconsistent reporting and fluctuating taxable income had not built the foundation he imagined. The estimated amount would barely cover basic housing in his city. For the first time, retirement stopped feeling abstract and became mathematical.

He responded the way many capable people do. He tried to increase his workload. He accepted smaller gigs he once would have declined. He drove farther, stacked multiple performances into single weekends, and said yes to opportunities that left him exhausted. Yet the additional effort did not produce the acceleration he hoped for. Market rates had shifted. Energy mattered more than it once did. Recovery time lengthened. The strategy of simply "working more" was no longer as reliable as it had been in his thirties and forties.

One afternoon, after losing a long-standing residency that had anchored his income for years, William began researching financial apps on his phone. He explored retirement accounts and high-yield savings platforms. As he reviewed his balances and compared them to what he might realistically need if he lived into his eighties or beyond, he felt something heavier than panic. He felt disorientation. He was approaching sixty with no meaningful retirement account, modest Social Security benefits, no pension, no property, and no structured long-term plan.

For decades, he had sustained himself successfully from year to year. That approach worked as long as bookings remained steady and his health cooperated. What he had not fully considered was the possibility of living twenty or thirty years beyond his peak earning period without structural reserves beneath him. The realization was not dramatic, but it was sobering. He began to understand that income and security are not the same thing. Income fluctuates. Security is built.

William's profession is not the point. His pattern is.
Across industries and income levels, many capable adults reach their late fifties or early sixties having built careers but not financial foundations. They built reputations but not reserves. They built skill but not structure. They relied on momentum. Momentum works—until time interrupts it.

William was not irresponsible. He worked hard. He adapted. He sustained himself for decades. But flexibility had replaced structure, and flexibility does not automatically convert into long-term stability. As he approached sixty, he recognized that continuing without deliberate strategy would gradually narrow his options. The fear was not immediate collapse. It was erosion. It was the slow reduction of flexibility as time advanced.

He began to imagine two possible futures. In one, he continued drifting from engagement to engagement, hoping his health held and the market remained kind enough to sustain him. In the other, he confronted the numbers honestly and redesigned his financial life, even if that meant redefining what retirement would look like. The second path required humility, clarity, and decisive action.

The first required hope.

Hope, he was beginning to realize, was not a strategy.

He was not beyond recovery. He still had earning capacity. He still had experience. He still had the ability to adjust. What he no longer had was unlimited time. That recognition marked the beginning of his financial awakening. And that awakening is where the No Money Nightmare truly begins.

TWO
WHEN INCOME FEELS LIKE SECURITY

William's story is not unusual. In fact, it is more common than most people are willing to admit. The details may differ from person to person, but the underlying pattern is the same. For years, income flows in. Bills get paid. Life moves forward. There is no immediate crisis, so there is no immediate urgency. The absence of disaster begins to feel like proof of stability.

But income and stability are not the same thing.

Income is movement. It is money arriving and money leaving. Stability is structure. It is what remains when income slows down. Many people mistake the steady arrival of checks for long-term security. As long as money continues to circulate through their hands, they assume they are financially solid. The problem only becomes visible when that circulation weakens.

For decades, William relied on his ability to generate income. If a slow month arrived, he booked more gigs. If an unexpected expense appeared, he found another event to play. His skill gave him confidence. His reputation gave him access. That pattern reinforced the belief that he could always solve financial pressure with effort.

That belief works - until it doesn't.

Income is active. It requires energy, opportunity, health, and demand. Stability, on the other hand, is passive. It does not require you to be at your peak every day. It does not depend entirely on the market choosing you. Stability is built in advance. It exists even when you are tired. It exists when the phone rings less often. It exists when the industry shifts.

When income feels steady for long enough, the mind begins to relax. You stop imagining worst-case scenarios. You stop calculating how long savings would last. You assume that next year will look similar to this year. The repetition of "good enough" years can quietly replace deliberate planning.

Many people who find themselves in a late-life financial squeeze did not spend recklessly. They simply relied too heavily on momentum. Momentum is powerful when you are young and in demand. It becomes fragile when time begins to narrow your options.

The illusion of security is comfortable because it removes pressure. As long as you are working and paying bills, you can postpone difficult questions. You can delay opening retirement statements. You can tell yourself that there will be time to adjust later. You can assume that your earning ability will naturally rise with experience.

For some professions, that assumption holds. For others, it does not. And even in stable industries, health and economic shifts can interrupt income without warning.

The difficult truth is that income alone does not guarantee safety in later years. Safety requires reserves. It requires systems. It requires something that continues working even when you are not.

William's awakening was not about a single bad year. It was about recognizing that he had built a career but not a foundation beneath it. He had built relationships and a reputation. What he had not built was anything that would keep functioning once he stepped off the stage.

That recognition is uncomfortable, but it is not fatal. In fact, it is necessary. The moment you distinguish between active income and structural security is the moment you begin to regain control. It forces you to examine whether your current lifestyle is supported by systems or sustained entirely by your continued effort.

If your lifestyle depends entirely on your ongoing energy and market demand, then your retirement plan is not yet a plan. It is a continuation of work. And that realization leads to the next question: why do so many capable, intelligent adults avoid building structure until it becomes urgent?

THREE
THE AVOIDANCE PATTERN

Financial avoidance rarely looks dramatic. It does not announce itself loudly. It appears in small decisions repeated over time. It shows up when you choose not to log into an account because the number makes you uneasy. It shows up when you assume Social Security will somehow cover more than it realistically will. It shows up when you promise yourself that you will "get serious next year."

Avoidance is not laziness. It is discomfort management.
Most people do not avoid retirement planning because they are unintelligent. They avoid it because it forces them to confront aging, limitation, and uncertainty. It requires admitting that time is not infinite. It asks you to project yourself decades forward and calculate what you might need when your earning capacity slows down.

For someone like William, the avoidance pattern was subtle. He did not wake up one morning and decide to ignore the future. He simply focused on what was immediately in front of him. Gigs needed to be secured. Equipment needed repair. Travel needed coordination. Each decision felt practical. Each year that passed without crisis reinforced the belief that he was managing well enough.

Avoidance becomes especially powerful when income is irregular. In fluctuating professions, financial discipline can feel almost unrealistic. When money comes in bursts, the instinct is to enjoy the strong periods and survive the weak ones. Long-term planning feels secondary to short-term stabilization.

There is also an emotional layer. Many independent workers tie their identity to their productivity. As long as they can produce, perform, consult, or create, they feel secure. Planning for retirement can feel like acknowledging decline. It can feel like admitting that someday you will not be the primary engine of your income. That thought is uncomfortable, so it is postponed.

Another layer of avoidance comes from complexity. Retirement accounts, tax planning, Social Security optimization, and investment terminology can feel overwhelming. When something feels complicated, the mind often defaults to inaction. It is easier to continue familiar habits than to learn a new financial system late in life.

Over time, avoidance creates a widening gap between reality and assumption. The longer the gap exists, the more intimidating it becomes to confront. By the late fifties or early sixties, many people suspect that they are behind, but they do not know by how much. Instead of calculating the difference, they rely on hope, extended work years, or vague plans to "figure it out."

Hope has emotional value, but it does not reduce financial risk. Extended work years can help, but only if health and opportunity cooperate. Vague plans rarely survive unexpected events.

The turning point comes when discomfort outweighs denial. For William, that moment arrived when he saw his projected Social Security benefit and realized it would not sustain his current lifestyle. The number forced clarity. It interrupted the comfort of assumption.

Avoidance is powerful because it protects your emotions in the short term. It allows you to preserve confidence. It delays anxiety. But it quietly widens the gap between where you are and where you need to be. A pivot point is only useful if you take the turn. If you see yourself in William's hesitation - in his delayed planning, in his assumption that income would always compensate for structure - you are not alone. Many intelligent, hardworking individuals arrive at this realization later than they intended.

The purpose of this book is not to criticize that delay. It is to help you respond to it. Once avoidance ends, strategy can begin. Once the numbers are acknowledged, they can be addressed. Once the illusion of security is replaced with honest assessment, real stability can be built. The next step is to examine the numbers clearly and understand where you truly stand. Only then can you determine how to close the gap between your current reality and the stability you need for the years ahead.

PART TWO

THE AWAKENING

FOUR
THE RETIREMENT STORY WE WERE SOLD

Most of us did not invent our expectations about retirement. We inherited them.

For decades, a quiet cultural script shaped the way Americans viewed later life. The script was simple and reassuring. Work hard. Buy a home. Contribute to a retirement account. Reach sixty-five. Retire. Relax. The formula felt dependable. It suggested that discipline would naturally lead to comfort.

That script worked reasonably well for a specific generation under specific conditions. Stable corporate employment was more common. Pensions were widely available. Healthcare costs were lower relative to income. Housing appreciation created significant equity for many homeowners. Life expectancy after retirement was shorter, meaning retirement savings did not need to last as long.

But economic conditions changed. Employment became less predictable. Pensions largely disappeared and were replaced by self-managed retirement accounts. Healthcare costs increased significantly.

Housing prices rose faster than wages in many areas. Individuals began living longer, often well into their eighties and nineties.

The cultural script did not evolve as quickly as reality did. Many people continued following the formula without recognizing that the underlying environment had shifted. They worked hard. They purchased homes. They contributed when they could. But irregular income, family responsibilities, recessions, health events, and wage stagnation interrupted consistency. By the time retirement approached, the math did not fully support the expectation.

The uncomfortable truth is that a large percentage of Americans are not on track to retire comfortably. This is not a reflection of laziness or irresponsibility. It is often the result of structural shifts that outpaced individual planning. Yet the dominant financial messaging continues to emphasize accumulation strategies designed for people who start early and remain consistent for thirty or forty years.

It is easy to write a book that says, "Invest two hundred dollars a month for thirty years and you will build substantial wealth." It is far more difficult to write a book for someone who is sixty-one with forty thousand dollars saved and ask, "Now what?"

The financial industry naturally focuses on growth narratives. Stories about early retirement, millionaire mindsets, scaling income, and aggressive investing are easier to market. Recovery stories are quieter. They require adjustment rather than expansion. They involve housing changes, expense compression, delayed gratification, and extended work horizons. Those solutions are practical but not glamorous.

The result is a gap in the conversation. Many individuals in their late fifties and early sixties feel behind, but they rarely see themselves reflected in mainstream financial guidance. They are not looking to become millionaires. They are looking to avoid instability. They are seeking control, not luxury.

There is also a psychological layer that makes this conversation difficult. Admitting that you are financially underprepared in later life can trigger embarrassment. It can feel like an indictment of decades of effort. People may compare themselves to peers who appear more secure and assume they alone miscalculated. This quiet comparison reinforces silence.

Shame is one of the most powerful forces keeping this subject hidden. Many individuals in their late fifties and sixties do not openly discuss being behind. They continue presenting confidence in social settings while privately running numbers at night. They do not walk into bookstores asking for help in rebuilding late-life stability. They hope something will improve on its own.
Silence does not solve structural imbalance.

It is harder to give hope in this context without exaggerating outcomes. It would be dishonest to promise that every late starter can retire comfortably without meaningful adjustments. It would also be dishonest to suggest that the situation is hopeless. The truth lies between those extremes. Recovery is possible, but it requires lifestyle changes, ego adjustments, housing reconsideration, extended income generation, and a redefinition of retirement itself.

Retirement does not have to mean the complete absence of work. It does not have to mean travel and leisure funded entirely by passive income. For many, retirement becomes financial stability, reduced stress, controlled expenses, strategic income, and the absence of catastrophic decline. That version of retirement is not widely advertised, but it is realistic and attainable with deliberate action.

Healthcare realities must also be confronted. Even with Medicare, out-of-pocket expenses, supplemental plans, prescriptions, and long-term care considerations can significantly impact cash flow. Medical events are not rare exceptions in later life; they are statistical probabilities. Planning must account for this reality. Ignoring healthcare cost inflation is one of the fastest ways to destabilize an otherwise balanced retirement plan.

Longevity adds another layer of complexity. If you retire at sixty-seven and live until ninety, your financial structure must support twenty-three years without full-time income. If you live to ninety-five, that period extends even further. Many people underestimate how long their resources must last. Living longer is a gift, but it requires preparation. The risk is not dying too soon; it is outliving your money.

When you combine longer lifespans, rising healthcare costs, housing inflation, and irregular employment histories, it becomes clear why the traditional retirement narrative does not fit everyone. Recognizing this mismatch is not pessimism. It is realism.

The purpose of confronting the retirement story we were sold is not to create resentment. It is to replace outdated assumptions with informed strategy. Once you accept that the old script may not fully apply to you, you are free to design a new one.

That design may include downsizing aggressively, relocating to a lower-cost region, increasing structured income for five to ten additional years, converting home equity into income-producing stability, delaying Social Security strategically, compressing recurring expenses, building small but consistent revenue streams, and prioritizing health as a financial asset. None of these moves are glamorous. All of them are powerful.

Recovery is not a growth story. It is a stabilization story. It is not about catching up to someone else's timeline. It is about strengthening your own structure before time reduces your options.

If you are reading this and recognizing yourself in these pages, you are not alone, and you are not beyond recovery. You are simply confronting reality at a moment when clarity matters most. That clarity is not a sentence. It is a starting point.

The American retirement dream was not entirely false. It was incomplete.

The promise of working hard, buying a home, saving steadily, and retiring at sixty-five did work under specific economic conditions. But those conditions were not permanent. Pensions declined. Healthcare costs rose. Wages stagnated relative to housing and education. Lifespans extended. The structure shifted, yet the messaging remained simple.

The problem was not the dream itself. The problem was assuming the dream required no adaptation. When economic reality changes, strategy must change with it. Clinging to an outdated script does not preserve dignity. It increases risk.
You are not betraying the dream by adjusting it. You are modernizing it.

FIVE
THE QUIET PANIC NOBODY TALKS ABOUT

There is a specific kind of fear that does not show up in conversation. It does not announce itself at dinner parties. It does not trend on social media. It does not become a public confession. It shows up late at night, when the house is quiet and the mind is not distracted. It shows up when you log into an account and stare at a number that feels smaller than it should be. It shows up when someone casually mentions retiring at sixty-two and you smile politely while calculating whether that could ever apply to you.

This fear is not dramatic. It is quiet. It is steady. It is the realization that time is no longer theoretical.

For many men and women in their late fifties and early sixties, the panic is not about poverty tomorrow. It is about erosion. It is about the slow narrowing of options. It is about wondering whether health will cooperate long enough to work five more years. It is about noticing that energy is not what it was at forty-five. It is about realizing that if income slows down, there is no deep reservoir beneath it.

Shame amplifies this panic.

Men often tie identity to provision. Professionals tie identity to competence. Creative workers tie identity to relevance. Admitting that your retirement structure is thin can feel like admitting you miscalculated life itself. It can feel like a personal failure rather than a structural reality. So the subject stays hidden. Conversations remain surface-level. You present confidence publicly while privately running numbers in your head.

The silence reinforces isolation. You assume others are further ahead. You assume you are the exception. You assume you should have known better.

But the truth is far less dramatic and far more common.

A significant percentage of Americans in this age range are underprepared for retirement. Many are severely underprepared. They are not reckless people. They are not unintelligent. They are people who lived through economic shifts, wage stagnation, disappearing pensions, rising healthcare costs, family obligations, and unpredictable markets. They worked. They adapted. They survived. But survival is not the same as long-term structure.

The quiet panic nobody talks about is not weakness. It is awareness breaking through denial. And awareness, though uncomfortable, is the beginning of power. The moment you name the panic, it loses some of its control over you. The moment you measure your position, you begin reclaiming leverage.

You are not behind because you are incapable. You are behind because the system changed and no one rewrote the script loudly enough. Now you are rewriting it for yourself.

SIX
THE COST OF DRIFTING

There is a difference between struggling and drifting. Struggling is active. It involves effort, response, and movement. Drifting is passive. It is what happens when important decisions are postponed long enough that time begins making them for you.

Many people in their late fifties and early sixties are not in crisis. They are drifting. Drifting looks calm on the surface. The bills are paid. Work continues. Life functions. But beneath that surface, no structural adjustments are being made. The retirement gap remains unmeasured or unaddressed. Housing costs remain unchanged even if they are misaligned with projected income. Social Security timing is left to convenience rather than strategy. Income expansion is discussed but not designed.

Drift feels safe because nothing dramatic is happening. Yet drift carries a cost.

If your monthly burn rate exceeds your projected guaranteed income by $1,500, that represents an $18,000 annual shortfall. Over ten years, that gap becomes $180,000. Over twenty years, it becomes $360,000.

These are not abstract figures. They represent pressure that must be absorbed by continued earning capacity, by asset withdrawals, or by future lifestyle reduction. If nothing changes, your options narrow gradually rather than suddenly. Your energy becomes more valuable than your assets. You work longer than you intended, not by preference but by necessity. You delay important decisions until they become urgent. You accept financial tension as normal background noise.

Drift rarely ends in dramatic collapse. It ends in constraint. Constraint appears as working because you must rather than because you choose to. It appears as postponing healthcare decisions to preserve cash flow. It appears as maintaining a lifestyle that quietly strains your future self. It appears as hoping inflation does not rise faster than your income, or that your health holds longer than the math requires. None of this happens overnight. That is precisely what makes drifting so dangerous. It erodes options slowly, quietly, and without warning signs.

The uncomfortable truth is that if you do nothing different between fifty-five and sixty-five, the math will not improve on its own. Time does not automatically close retirement gaps. Markets do not reliably compensate for lack of structure. Social Security does not replace a lifestyle built primarily on active income. Hope may feel emotionally reassuring, but it is financially neutral. Without structural change, the trajectory remains the same.

This chapter is not written to frighten you. It is written to interrupt passivity. If you recognize yourself in this pattern, you are not failing. You are at a decision point. You still possess earning capacity. You still have the ability to compress expenses, restructure housing, expand income intelligently, and optimize benefits. Leverage decreases with time, however. Five intentional years can meaningfully alter your financial trajectory. Five unstructured years can permanently narrow the choices available to you.

The cost of drifting is not dramatic ruin. It is a gradual loss of flexibility. And flexibility, in later life, is power. This book exists to prevent that quiet erosion — not to judge the path that brought you here, but to interrupt the one that lies ahead if nothing changes.

If you feel the tightening of reality, that is not panic. It is awareness. And awareness, once it arrives, is the moment just before deliberate design.

PART THREE

THE REALITY CHECK

SEVEN
WHERE YOU ACTUALLY STAND

Before you can redesign your later years, you must know exactly where you are. Not where you hoped you would be. Not where you assumed you were. Not where you tell others you are. You must know your real position.

This is not an emotional exercise. It is a clarity exercise.
Many people avoid this step because they fear what they might discover. They assume that if the numbers are disappointing, facing them will make the situation worse. The opposite is true. Ignoring unclear numbers creates instability. Clear numbers create options.

The goal in this chapter is not to judge your past decisions. It is to assess your current stability. Once you see the structure clearly, you can adjust it. Until you see it clearly, you are operating on assumptions.

There are six areas you must examine.

The first is your monthly burn rate. This is the amount of money it takes to run your life each month. Not your ideal budget. Not your emergency version. Your real, current lifestyle cost. Include housing, utilities, food, transportation, insurance, healthcare, subscriptions, and discretionary spending. Do not guess. Review actual statements. Most people underestimate this number. Stability begins with accuracy.

The second is your guaranteed income. Guaranteed income includes Social Security, pensions, annuities, or any predictable payment that does not depend on you working. If you are not yet receiving Social Security, review your projected benefit at different claiming ages. Understand what the numbers truly are, not what you assume they might be.

The third area is the income gap. Subtract your guaranteed income from your monthly burn rate. If your expenses are $4,000 per month and your guaranteed income is projected to be $2,000, then you have a $2,000 monthly gap. This number is not meant to frighten you. It is meant to clarify the challenge. Many people feel anxious because they sense a gap but have never calculated it precisely. Once it is calculated, it becomes a problem that can be addressed.

The fourth area is your assets. Assets include retirement accounts, savings, brokerage accounts, home equity, and any other property with financial value. List them clearly. Do not round up optimistically. Do not assume future appreciation. Record what exists today. Liquidity matters. Assets that can be converted into usable stability are different from assets that are emotionally attached but financially idle.

The fifth area is debt. Mortgage balances, credit cards, car loans, personal loans, and tax obligations all affect your stability. Debt is not automatically catastrophic, but it changes the pressure on your monthly cash flow. A high monthly burn combined with high debt reduces flexibility. Knowing your total obligations allows you to see whether restructuring is necessary.

The sixth area is time. Time is the most overlooked financial variable. How many working years do you realistically have left? Not how many you hope for, but how many your health, industry, and energy likely support. If you are fifty-eight, you may have ten productive years ahead. If you are sixty-five, that window may be narrower. Time determines how aggressively you must act and how much leverage you still have.

When you review these six areas honestly, something important happens. The anxiety that once felt vague becomes specific. Specific problems are easier to solve than undefined fear.

If your monthly burn rate exceeds your guaranteed income significantly, then you know you must either reduce expenses, increase reliable income, or adjust housing. If your assets are minimal but you still have earning years, then the strategy shifts toward acceleration and structure. If you have strong assets but high expenses, then optimization becomes the focus.

Clarity does not guarantee comfort. It guarantees direction.
Some readers will discover that their situation is not as severe as they feared. Others will realize they are further behind than they expected. Both outcomes are valuable. Overestimating your stability leads to complacency. Underestimating it leads to paralysis. Accurate assessment leads to strategy.

You are not evaluating yourself as a person. You are evaluating your structure.

If the structure is weak, it can be reinforced. If it is unbalanced, it can be adjusted. If it is incomplete, it can be built.
The goal of this book is not to promise a luxurious retirement. It is to help you build sustainable stability. Sustainable stability begins with knowing exactly where you stand today.

In the next chapter, we will examine the retirement gap more closely and understand what it truly means, not as a source of fear, but as a problem that can be measured and managed.

EIGHT
UNDERSTANDING THE RETIREMENT GAP

Once you have calculated your monthly burn rate and your projected guaranteed income, you are ready to face one of the most important numbers in this entire process: the retirement gap.
The retirement gap is not a moral judgment. It is not a reflection of your intelligence or discipline. It is simply the difference between what your life costs and what your guaranteed income will provide.

If your monthly expenses are $3,800 and your projected guaranteed income from Social Security and other sources is $2,100, then your retirement gap is $1,700 per month. That gap does not mean you have failed. It means there is a structural imbalance that must be addressed.

Many people avoid calculating this number because they assume it will be overwhelming. In reality, the absence of a number creates more anxiety than the number itself. When the gap is undefined, it feels limitless. When it is defined, it becomes measurable.
Let us look at a neutral example.

Assume a sixty-year-old individual has the following financial picture. Their current monthly expenses total $4,200. Their projected Social

Security benefit at full retirement age is $2,000 per month. They have $85,000 saved in retirement accounts and $20,000 in a savings account. They carry a remaining mortgage balance of $120,000 on a home valued at $325,000.

Their retirement gap at age sixty-seven would be $2,200 per month if they made no adjustments.

At first glance, that gap appears intimidating. But clarity allows strategy. If they withdrew $2,200 per month from their retirement savings to cover the difference, that would equal $26,400 per year. At that rate, $105,000 in combined liquid assets would not last many years, especially when market fluctuations and inflation are considered.

This is where many people become discouraged. They see that the math does not support maintaining their current lifestyle indefinitely, and they assume the situation is hopeless.
It is not hopeless. It is incomplete.

The retirement gap is not a signal to panic. It is a signal to adjust one or more variables. There are only three ways to close a gap: reduce expenses, increase reliable income, or restructure assets. Sometimes the solution involves all three.

If expenses are reduced from $4,200 to $3,200 through downsizing, debt reduction, or relocation, the gap shrinks immediately. If guaranteed income is increased by delaying Social Security or adding structured part-time work, the gap narrows further. If housing equity is repositioned to reduce monthly costs, pressure decreases significantly. The gap is not static. It responds to decisions.

It is also important to understand that retirement is no longer a fixed moment. For many people, retirement becomes a phased transition rather than a hard stop. A smaller income gap can often be covered by modest, flexible work that is less demanding than a full-time career.

The goal is not necessarily to eliminate all work immediately, but to remove instability.

Another critical factor is longevity. Many people underestimate how long their resources must last. A person retiring at sixty-seven may need their financial structure to support them for twenty-five or even thirty years. That reality makes the retirement gap more significant, not less. However, it also reinforces why early clarity matters. The sooner you identify the gap, the more options you preserve.

Some readers will discover that their gap is smaller than they feared. Others will find it larger. Neither result changes the core principle: unmeasured gaps create anxiety, measured gaps create strategy.

The retirement gap is not your enemy. It is a diagnostic tool. It reveals the difference between your current lifestyle and your projected support structure. Once you understand it clearly, you can begin adjusting the components that influence it.

In the next chapter, we will examine the levers you still control, even at this stage of life. You may not be able to rewrite the past, but you can still adjust housing, income structure, expenses, and asset positioning. These levers determine whether the gap remains overwhelming or becomes manageable.

NINE
HEALTHCARE AND LONGEVITY

Healthcare is not a peripheral expense in retirement. It is one of the central variables.

Even with Medicare, premiums, supplemental policies, prescriptions, deductibles, and out-of-pocket costs can create significant monthly pressure. A single unexpected medical event can shift annual expenses by thousands of dollars. Long-term care - whether at home or in a facility - can dramatically alter the financial picture if not planned for in advance.

Healthcare inflation historically rises faster than general inflation. That means the purchasing power of your retirement income may decline more rapidly in the medical category than in others. Ignoring this reality creates structural weakness.

Longevity compounds the challenge. If you retire at sixty-seven and live to ninety, your structure must support twenty-three years of living expenses. If you live to ninety-five, it must support nearly three decades. The risk in modern retirement is rarely dying too early. It is outliving your money.

This is why health preservation must be viewed as a financial strategy. Preventive care, strength maintenance, mobility, and stress management are not simply quality-of-life decisions. They protect earning capacity. They reduce catastrophic risk. They preserve optionality.

In later life, health and money are not separate conversations. They are intertwined variables in the same equation.

TEN
THE LEVERS YOU STILL CONTROL

If you have made it this far, you have already done something many people never do. You have faced the numbers. You have calculated your burn rate. You have identified your guaranteed income. You have measured your retirement gap. That alone puts you ahead of the majority of individuals drifting toward later life without clarity.

Now it is time to shift your perspective.

The retirement gap may feel heavy, but it is not a wall. It is a gap between two points, and gaps can be closed. The key is understanding that you still control several powerful levers. Even in your late fifties or sixties, you are not without influence. You are not without options. You are not out of time unless you decide to remain passive.

The first and most powerful lever is housing. For most people, housing is the single largest monthly expense. It is also often the largest asset. Adjusting housing can dramatically alter your financial structure. Downsizing, relocating to a lower-cost area, refinancing, renting out a portion of your home, or transitioning from ownership to a more manageable living arrangement can reduce your burn rate immediately. A reduction of even $800 to $1,200 per month changes the entire retirement equation. Housing is not just where you live; it is a financial engine that can either drain you or stabilize you.

The second lever is income structure. Notice the word structure. This is not about working yourself into exhaustion. It is about designing income intentionally. Part-time consulting, seasonal work, remote service-based roles, tutoring, event-based work, property management, creative monetization, or small business adjustments can add controlled supplemental income. Even an additional $1,000 per month reduces a $2,000 gap by half. When income is designed rather than reactive, it becomes stabilizing instead of stressful.

The third lever is benefit optimization. Many individuals underestimate the power of timing. Delaying Social Security increases your monthly benefit significantly. Understanding spousal benefits, survivor benefits, and taxation thresholds can add meaningful stability. This requires education, not guesswork. Strategic timing is not gambling; it is math applied with patience.

The fourth lever is expense compression. This does not mean living in deprivation. It means examining which expenses are attached to ego, habit, or convenience rather than necessity. Subscriptions, underused services, oversized vehicles, high-interest debt, and lifestyle inflation accumulate quietly. Reducing your monthly burn rate by $500 or $700 may not sound dramatic, but over ten years it is transformative. Every dollar removed from recurring expense reduces the pressure on your future self.

The fifth lever is asset repositioning. Idle assets do not create stability. Underused property, excess vehicles, collectibles, equipment, or inherited items may hold emotional value but little strategic value. In some cases, converting idle assets into liquid reserves or income-producing tools creates breathing room. Stability often increases when assets are aligned with purpose rather than nostalgia.

The sixth lever is health. Health is financial leverage. Medical instability can erase years of planning. Investing in preventive care, movement, nutrition, and stress management is not separate from financial planning. It is part of it. The longer you maintain functional health, the more control you retain over income options and expenses.

When William finally confronted his numbers, he initially felt cornered. But once he understood these levers, his situation looked different. He realized that his lifestyle was not fixed. He could relocate to a lower-cost city where his industry contacts still provided occasional work. He could transition from late-night event performances to teaching and studio work. He could restructure his expenses to reflect the stage of life he was entering instead of the stage he was leaving. None of those adjustments were dramatic. But combined, they were powerful.

The mistake many people make is believing that recovery requires one massive breakthrough. It rarely does. Stability is built through layered adjustments. A smaller home. A redesigned income stream. Smarter benefit timing. Lower recurring expenses. Health discipline. Together, these shifts can transform a frightening gap into a manageable plan.

You may not be able to rebuild thirty years of missed savings. But you can redesign the next ten years with precision. Ten intentional years can radically change your trajectory. Five intentional years can protect you from collapse. Even twelve intentional months can restore control.

Possibility does not mean fantasy. It means movement. It means recognizing that you are not locked into your current structure. You are only locked into it if you refuse to adjust it.

The No Money Nightmare loses power the moment you begin pulling the levers available to you. Awareness becomes strategy. Strategy becomes action. Action becomes stability.

In the next section, we will move from possibility into implementation. You will not need complex financial expertise. You will need discipline, clarity, and a willingness to act. The next twelve months can either continue the drift or begin the reset.
The choice is still yours.

The Acceleration Window (55–62)

If you are between fifty-five and sixty-two, you are in what I call the Acceleration Window. This is not the beginning of retirement. It is the final phase of high-leverage decision-making. You still have earning capacity. You are still employable. You are still insurable. You still have physical and geographic flexibility that narrows significantly after your mid-sixties.

Five to seven intentional years at this stage can materially change your financial trajectory. Five years of generating two thousand dollars per month in supplemental income equals one hundred twenty thousand dollars before taxes. Combined with expense compression or housing restructuring, that window can close a meaningful portion of a retirement gap. The objective is not to eliminate every deficit. It is to reduce risk while expanding control.

This is the window where aggressive downsizing can free equity and permanently reduce your burn rate. It is the window where relocating to a lower-cost region can transform your monthly equation without requiring dramatic sacrifice. It is the window where structured income expansion - consulting, advisory work, part-time professional roles, skill monetization - can build reserves quickly while energy and market demand are still working in your favor. It is also the window where delaying Social Security strategically can permanently increase lifetime benefits, strengthening your guaranteed income base.

If you wait until sixty-seven or seventy to restructure, your options compress. Health variables increase. Energy narrows. The market becomes less forgiving. Relocation becomes harder. Insurance costs rise. The same actions are still possible - but they are less flexible and more constrained.

Acceleration does not mean panic. It means precision. It means recognizing that this stage of life is not about drifting toward retirement and hoping the numbers improve. It is about redirecting momentum while you still have room to maneuver.

Ten unfocused years disappear quickly. Five intentional years compound meaningfully. The Acceleration Window is not about regret for what was not done earlier. It is about disciplined leverage in the present, while leverage still exists.

PART FOUR

THE RESET

ELEVEN
THE INCOME REPOSITIONING BLUEPRINT

If you are between fifty-five and sixty-five and financially behind, the conversation cannot be limited to cutting expenses. Expense reduction creates breathing room, but income repositioning creates momentum. The goal at this stage of life is not explosive wealth. It is controlled, structured cash flow that reduces pressure and restores stability.

At this age, you are not starting from zero. You are starting from experience. You have accumulated decades of skill, judgment, pattern recognition, relationships, and lived insight. Those assets may not appear on a balance sheet, but they have value in the marketplace. The challenge is not whether you have value. The challenge is whether that value is being positioned correctly.

Income repositioning is different from career reinvention. Reinvention often requires long runways, steep learning curves, and significant risk. Repositioning leverages what you already know and translates it into structured income with lower volatility and lower ego attachment. At fifty-five to sixty-five, stability matters more than status.

There are four primary income lanes available in this stage of life: skill monetization, asset monetization, knowledge packaging, and stability-based part-time work. Most people will combine two or more of these lanes rather than relying on a single stream.

The first lane is skill monetization. This is the most overlooked opportunity among experienced professionals. If you have spent twenty, thirty, or forty years in a field, you possess institutional knowledge that younger professionals do not. Companies often need guidance without committing to full-time salaries. Consulting, advisory roles, project-based contracts, fractional leadership positions, mentoring, or training can provide meaningful income without the physical demands of traditional employment.

Consider a former operations manager who offers process improvement consulting at seventy-five dollars per hour for fifteen hours per week. That produces roughly four thousand five hundred dollars per month before taxes. Even at a lower rate of fifty dollars per hour for ten hours per week, that still generates two thousand dollars per month. That income alone can significantly reduce a retirement gap.

The second lane is asset monetization. Many people underestimate the value of assets they already control. Housing is the most powerful lever. Renting a finished basement, an accessory dwelling unit, or even a single room can produce eight hundred to one thousand dollars per month in many markets. That represents nine to twelve thousand dollars per year in additional income without creating a new career. Downsizing and investing the difference between mortgage costs and rental expenses can also reposition monthly cash flow. Equipment, vehicles, storage space, land, or specialized tools may generate supplemental income if structured properly.

The third lane is knowledge packaging. This does not require becoming an influencer. It involves organizing your experience into usable formats. Workshops, online classes, local seminars, digital guides, niche consulting packages, or instructional material can create modest but consistent income streams. A retired human resources executive might offer interview coaching packages. A former teacher might create curriculum support sessions for parents. A tradesperson might teach safety workshops or technical basics. Knowledge that once earned a salary can often earn fees when packaged correctly.

The fourth lane is stability-based part-time work. This lane requires humility but offers reliability. Universities, hospitals, local government offices, nonprofit organizations, and established corporations frequently hire part-time administrative, coordination, mentoring, or support roles. These roles may not carry the prestige of prior titles, but they provide structured income with predictable hours and lower volatility. Stability-based income is not a step backward. It is a strategic move toward reduced pressure.

One of the most important mental adjustments at this stage is separating income from identity. Many individuals resist certain income opportunities because they perceive them as beneath their previous status. This resistance is understandable but costly. At fifty-five to sixty-five, income is about structure, not ego. A two-thousand-dollar monthly stream that reduces anxiety and preserves savings is powerful, regardless of the job title attached to it.

Delaying Social Security can also function as an income strategy. If you can generate part-time or consulting income between sixty-two and sixty-seven, you increase your eventual monthly benefit permanently. That decision compounds over decades. Structured income now can produce higher guaranteed income later.

The objective of income repositioning is not to recreate your peak earning years. It is to build a bridge between your current position and long-term stability. A combination of two modest streams - for example, a one-thousand-dollar rental income and a two-thousand-dollar consulting contract - can generate thirty-six thousand dollars per year. Over five intentional years, that represents one hundred eighty thousand dollars before taxes. That level of structured income can dramatically change the trajectory of your retirement math.

Momentum reduces panic. Structure reduces shame. Income repositioning restores control.

The key is to act deliberately rather than reactively. Identify your strongest skill. Identify one asset that can be repositioned. Identify one stability-based option that provides dependable income. Design your mix. Test it. Adjust it. Refine it. Income at this stage is not about speed. It is about sustainability.

You are not too late to create cash flow. You are too late to drift. The earlier you reposition your value, the longer that value works for you.

A Simple 90-Day Income Activation Plan

Clarity without action creates frustration. Action without structure creates exhaustion. The goal of the next ninety days is not perfection. It is activation. You are not trying to redesign your entire financial life in three months. You are trying to establish one or two controlled income streams that begin reducing pressure immediately.

Days 1–14 should be dedicated to inventory and decision. During this period, write down every skill you have used professionally for more than five years. List processes you understand deeply. List problems you know how to solve. Then list every tangible asset you control, including housing space, equipment, certifications, licenses, vehicles, tools, or intellectual property. Once this list is complete, choose one skill-based opportunity and one asset-based opportunity that feel realistic rather than idealistic. The key word is realistic. Avoid options that require extensive retraining or high startup costs.

Days 15–30 should focus on positioning. If you are pursuing consulting or skill monetization, draft a simple one-page description of the service you offer. It does not need to be elaborate. It needs to be clear. Identify who needs this service and how you will reach them. This may involve contacting former colleagues, local businesses, professional associations, or community networks. If you are pursuing asset monetization, use this period to prepare the asset for income use. Clean the space. Clarify rental terms. Research local pricing. Ensure compliance with local regulations. Action at this stage should be visible and measurable.

Days 31–60 are for outreach and testing. Make direct contact. Send emails. Make phone calls. Schedule conversations. List the rental. Advertise the service. Offer a limited introductory rate if needed to secure initial clients. This phase requires courage more than complexity. Many people stall here because they overthink. The objective is not to build a brand. It is to secure your first revenue.

Days 61–90 are for stabilization. Once the first income begins, refine the process. Adjust pricing if necessary. Clarify expectations. Improve efficiency. Document the steps that worked. If one lane proves ineffective, pivot quickly to the second option you identified in the first fourteen days. By day ninety, you should have at least one functioning income stream generating consistent cash flow, even if modest.

A modest stream matters. An additional one thousand to two thousand dollars per month can significantly reduce a retirement gap. It can preserve savings. It can allow you to delay Social Security strategically. It can restore psychological stability.

The ninety-day activation plan is not about speed. It is about breaking inertia. Once income begins flowing through a new structure, momentum replaces panic. You stop asking whether recovery is possible and start refining what is already working.
Three months from now, you will either have activated new income or you will have postponed again. The difference between those outcomes is not intelligence. It is decision.

A Real-World Illustration

Consider Linda, age fifty-nine. She spent thirty-two years as a mid-level operations manager for a regional distribution company. When the company restructured, her position was eliminated. She found another role, but at a lower salary. Her retirement savings were modest, and her Social Security projection would not fully cover her monthly expenses. She did not need a new career. She needed structured supplemental income.

During her first fourteen days, she listed her core skills: workflow optimization, vendor negotiation, team coordination, and compliance management. She also listed her assets: a paid-off home with a finished basement and a strong professional network from decades in logistics.

By day thirty, she had drafted a simple consulting offer focused on small businesses lacking operational systems. She reached out to former colleagues and local business owners, offering short-term process assessments at a flat introductory rate. At the same time, she prepared her basement for rental and researched comparable rates in her area.

The first two weeks of outreach were discouraging. She sent fourteen emails and received three responses, two of which were polite declines. She began to wonder whether her offer was unclear, whether her rates were wrong, or whether the whole approach was a mistake. On day twenty-two, she rewrote her outreach message, making it shorter and more direct about the specific problem she solved. Within a week, she had two interested conversations.

Between days thirty and sixty, she secured two small consulting engagements at seventy-five dollars per hour for ten hours each. That produced $1,500 in her first month of activation. She also rented her basement for $850 per month to a traveling nurse on a six-month agreement.

By day ninety, Linda had established approximately $2,350 per month in additional income - $28,200 annually before taxes. She did not change careers. She did not return to school. She did not take on physically demanding work. She repositioned experience and leveraged an existing asset.

That additional income allowed her to reduce withdrawals from her retirement account and delay claiming Social Security. Over five intentional years, this structure could preserve more than $100,000 in savings while increasing her eventual guaranteed benefit.

What made the difference was not the first attempt. It was the willingness to adjust it.

Consider David, age sixty-one. He worked for nearly thirty-five years as a licensed electrician. His income had always been solid. During strong construction cycles, he earned well. During slower periods, he relied on smaller residential jobs. He owned his home but had modest retirement savings and no pension. His Social Security projection would cover only a portion of his monthly expenses. The larger concern was physical strain. Long hours in tight spaces and heavy lifting were becoming more difficult.

During his first fourteen days of inventory, David listed not just his technical skill but his diagnostic ability. He realized that much of his value was not in physically installing wiring but in identifying problems quickly and advising on solutions. He also recognized that many younger electricians lacked business knowledge about estimating, pricing, and managing clients.

Structuring a new kind of service felt awkward at first. David had spent decades showing up, doing the work, and getting paid. The idea of charging for a conversation - for knowledge rather than labor - did not come naturally. His first two inspection appointments were priced too low because he second-guessed whether anyone would pay more.

He undercharged by nearly thirty percent before a peer in his network told him his rates were well below the local market.

He adjusted. By day thirty, David had restructured his service around paid electrical inspections, safety evaluations, and project consultations for homeowners and small contractors. He set flat fees for assessments and hourly rates for advisory work that reflected what the market actually supported. At the same time, he reached out to a local trade school and secured part-time instructional hours teaching code basics and job-site safety two evenings per week.

Between days thirty and sixty, he booked several inspection appointments and began teaching his first course. By day ninety, David had established approximately $2,800 per month in combined income from inspections, advisory work, and teaching. The physical strain was significantly lower than full construction labor, and his schedule was more predictable.

He did not abandon his trade. He repositioned it. Over five structured years, that level of supplemental income could generate more than $150,000 before taxes while preserving his physical health and delaying full retirement.

David's recovery did not come from working harder. It came from working differently - and from being willing to correct course once he realized he had started in the wrong direction.

Income at this stage of life is not about proving anything. It is about protecting your future self. It is about converting decades of experience into stability rather than allowing time to erode your options. The goal is not to recreate your peak earning years or compete with younger professionals on speed or scale. The goal is control. When you generate structured income intentionally, even in modest amounts, you reduce anxiety, preserve savings, strengthen your negotiating position with time, and reclaim dignity in the process. Repositioning income is not an admission of failure. It is an assertion of responsibility. And responsibility, exercised deliberately, restores power. The next step is to organize that power into a structured year-long reset.

TWELVE
THE 12-MONTH STABILITY RESET

You cannot change the past twenty years. You can change the next twelve months.

Twelve focused months can interrupt drift. They can reduce your burn rate, increase structured income, reposition assets, and restore control. This is not a fantasy rebuild. It is a disciplined reset designed for someone between fifty-five and sixty-five who still has earning capacity and decision power.

Recovery does not happen through intensity. It happens through structure. The purpose of the next twelve months is not to create dramatic transformation. It is to build stability deliberately and measurably. Twelve intentional months can change your trajectory more than five unstructured years.

Months 1–3: Activation and Clarity

The first ninety days are your activation window. This phase connects directly to the Income Repositioning Blueprint. During these three months, you inventory skills and assets, select one realistic income lane, and activate it. Your goal is not perfection. Your goal is movement. By the end of month three, you should have at least one functioning supplemental income stream generating consistent cash flow, even if modest. Simultaneously, you track your true monthly burn rate with precision. No estimates. No assumptions. Numbers create clarity. Clarity reduces anxiety.

Months 4–6: Structural Compression

Once income activation begins, the next priority is expense alignment. Review housing, transportation, subscriptions, insurance, and discretionary spending. Identify recurring expenses that do not meaningfully improve your quality of life. The objective is not deprivation. It is compression. Even a reduction of five hundred dollars per month equals six thousand dollars annually. Combined with new income streams, this phase often creates meaningful breathing room. If downsizing or relocation is under consideration, these months are when serious research and decision-making begin. Housing is not just a lifestyle choice. It is a financial engine.

Months 7–8: Housing and Asset Leverage

If housing adjustments are necessary, this is the implementation window. This may involve listing a property, preparing a rental unit, converting space for income use, or relocating to a lower-cost region. If relocation is not appropriate, focus on monetizing existing assets—rooms, storage, tools, vehicles, or other underutilized resources. Housing decisions often produce the single largest shift in retirement math. Acting deliberately in this phase can permanently lower your financial pressure.

Months 9–10: Benefit Strategy and Long-Term Positioning

This phase focuses on optimization rather than survival. Review your Social Security projections at different claiming ages. Compare the lifetime difference between claiming early and delaying. If your income repositioning has been successful, delaying benefits may now be realistic. Delayed benefits increase guaranteed lifetime income, which strengthens long-term stability. At this stage, evaluate debt reduction strategies, emergency fund targets, and retirement account contributions if possible. The objective is to strengthen your foundation, not merely sustain it.

Month 11: Health as Financial Strategy

Health is not separate from retirement planning. It is a financial variable. Use this month to schedule preventive medical appointments, assess physical fitness, and implement sustainable health habits that preserve earning capacity and reduce long-term risk. Improved strength, mobility, and stress management directly support income sustainability. Medical crises are expensive. Prevention is leverage.

Month 12: Review and Stabilization

The final month is for review. Compare your financial position at the start of the year to your position now. Calculate the reduction in your retirement gap. Document new income streams, reduced expenses, increased savings, and optimized benefits. Identify what worked and what requires adjustment. Stability is not a one-time event. It is a system that requires refinement. By the end of twelve months, you should not feel frantic. You should feel structured.

This twelve-month reset is not about catching up completely in one year. It is about changing direction. When direction changes early enough, trajectory changes with it. The difference between drifting and designing often begins with one deliberate year.
You cannot control the past. You can control the next twelve months. And twelve intentional months can restore more control than you think.

THIRTEEN
WILLIAM'S 12-MONTH RESET

When William first reviewed his numbers, he felt cornered. His projected Social Security benefit was lower than he expected, his retirement savings were minimal, and his income from performances had begun trending downward. For a few weeks, he felt overwhelmed by the realization that he had allowed structure to lag behind income for too many years. But instead of retreating into avoidance again, he committed to the reset.

In the first month, he gathered every financial document he could find. He reviewed his actual spending instead of relying on memory. His true monthly burn rate surprised him. It was higher than he believed, largely because of small recurring expenses and lifestyle habits built during stronger earning seasons. For the first time, he saw the full picture without filtering it through optimism.

In the second month, he focused on stabilization. He eliminated unused subscriptions, renegotiated his insurance, consolidated two high-interest credit cards, and set up a structured payment plan for back taxes he had delayed addressing. These changes did not transform his life overnight, but they reduced his monthly pressure by nearly four hundred dollars. The number was not dramatic, but it was real. The sense of control that came with it mattered more than the amount itself.

By the third and fourth months, he confronted his lifestyle honestly. He realized he was maintaining a standard of living designed for his peak earning years. He sold equipment he no longer used and redirected the proceeds toward debt reduction and a small emergency reserve. He replaced his leased vehicle with a reliable used car that carried no monthly payment. That decision alone reduced his burn rate by another five hundred dollars per month.

Months five and six marked a shift from defense to intention. Instead of chasing more late-night gigs that exhausted him, William restructured his income. He began offering private lessons and small group workshops during daytime hours. He partnered with a local community center to teach weekly sessions, creating predictable monthly income that did not depend on weekend demand. The income was modest compared to his peak performing years, but it was consistent and less physically demanding.

In month seven, he evaluated his housing. He had been renting in a higher-cost urban area close to venues he once played regularly. After careful analysis, he chose to relocate to a smaller city with lower rent and a slower pace. The move reduced his monthly housing cost by nearly eight hundred dollars. It also positioned him in a community where his experience was valued rather than overshadowed by younger competition.

Months eight and nine were about benefit strategy and structure. With his reduced burn rate and new supplemental income in place, William realized he could delay claiming Social Security longer than he initially thought. The increased projected benefit provided reassurance. He opened a structured retirement account for the first time in years and began contributing consistently, even if the amounts were modest. The act of contribution mattered as much as the balance.

By month ten, his emergency reserve was modest but present. He had repositioned idle assets and closed lingering financial leaks. For the first time in years, his financial life felt organized rather than reactive.

Months eleven and twelve focused on protection. He updated beneficiary designations, created a simple will, and clarified his medical directives. He scheduled preventive health appointments he had delayed. He began viewing his health not as a separate concern, but as part of his financial structure.

At the end of twelve months, William was not wealthy. His retirement accounts were still smaller than ideal. His Social Security benefit had not magically increased overnight. But his monthly burn rate had decreased by nearly one thousand dollars. His income structure was steadier. His debt was controlled. His housing cost was aligned with his reality. Most importantly, his retirement gap had narrowed to a manageable level.

The panic he once felt was replaced with measured confidence. He no longer relied solely on hope or momentum. He relied on structure.

William did not erase thirty years of informal planning in twelve months. He interrupted a dangerous trajectory. He replaced drift with design. He exchanged illusion for clarity.

His life did not become glamorous. It became stable.
And stability, at this stage of life, is a powerful form of freedom.

FOURTEEN
REDEFINING RETIREMENT

For decades, retirement has been presented as a destination - a fixed point that arrives after years of steady work and disciplined saving. The image is familiar: freedom from employment, reliable income, travel, leisure, and comfort. For some individuals, that version of retirement becomes reality. For many others, life unfolds differently. Careers shift. Health changes. Family responsibilities intervene. Income fluctuates. Time moves faster than expected. By the time many people pause to assess their situation in their late fifties or early sixties, they discover that their financial foundation is thinner than they once assumed.

That realization is not a verdict on your character. It is not proof that you were irresponsible or careless. It is a signal that your expectations must evolve.

Retirement is not defined by a birthday. It is not guaranteed by effort alone. It is not the automatic reward for reaching a certain age. At its core, retirement is financial stability - the ability to live without persistent fear about covering your basic expenses, to structure your income and control your costs, and to move through later life with steadiness rather than quiet dread.

If you are between fifty-five and sixty-five, you still possess meaningful leverage. You still have earning capacity, decision-making power, and time to adjust your trajectory. You may not be able to rebuild decades of missed contributions, but you can redesign the years ahead with clarity and intention. The purpose of this book has not been to promise luxury or early leisure. Its purpose has been to restore control.

The No Money Nightmare grows in vagueness and avoidance. It expands when assumptions go untested and numbers remain unexamined. It loses strength when you confront reality calmly and respond with deliberate action. Stability does not require dramatic transformation. It requires decisions made consistently: income repositioned, expenses aligned, benefits timed with intention, health preserved, housing leveraged wisely.

William's story, which has threaded through these pages, was not a story of sudden wealth or dramatic rescue. It was a story of recalibration - of replacing drift with design. His life did not become extravagant. It became manageable, and then it became stable. At this stage of life, that distinction matters more than most people expect. Stability reduces the constant background noise of financial fear. It gives you room to make choices rather than react to circumstances.

Your path forward will not mirror William's exactly. Your numbers are different. Your decisions may involve downsizing, relocating, continuing part-time work, consulting, selling assets, or building small but consistent income streams. These adjustments do not represent decline. They represent maturity. There is dignity in adapting your structure to your reality. There is strength in acknowledging where you stand and choosing to move forward with clarity rather than denial.

The next twelve months can meaningfully alter the trajectory of the next twenty years. Not because they erase the past, but because they align your future with practical truth. When your expenses are intentional, your income is structured, and your assets are positioned with purpose, the pressure that once felt overwhelming becomes manageable.

Retirement, redefined, is not withdrawal from life. It is deliberate design. It is choosing sustainability over appearance, structure over momentum, and preparation over hope.

You are not beyond recovery. You are not powerless. You are at a decision point. The steady, disciplined choices you make now can carry you further than you currently believe possible.

Stability is not built in a single dramatic moment. But it is built. One measured decision at a time, with clarity, with structure, and with the honest acknowledgment that leverage still exists - and that now is the time to use it.

That is not a small thing. That is enough.

PERSONAL STABILITY ASSESSMENT AND ACTION WORKSHEETS

This section is designed to move you from reflection into structured action. You have read the concepts. You have considered the scenarios. Now you will apply the framework directly to your own life. The purpose of these worksheets is not to overwhelm you. It is to create clarity and direction. You may complete them all at once or return to them gradually over several weeks. What matters most is honesty.

Where Am I Really? Stability Snapshot

Begin by writing down your current age and your intended retirement age, if you have one. If you do not have a specific retirement age in mind, write down the age at which you believe your full-time earning capacity may realistically slow down.

Next, calculate your true monthly burn rate. Review the past three months of bank and credit card statements and determine your average total monthly spending. Include housing, utilities, food, transportation, insurance, healthcare, debt payments, subscriptions, and discretionary spending. Write the total here.

Now, list your projected guaranteed monthly income at your intended retirement age. This includes Social Security, pensions, annuities, or any other predictable payments not dependent on active work. Write the projected total.

Subtract your guaranteed income from your monthly burn rate. The result is your retirement gap. Write that number clearly. This number is not a judgment. It is a starting point.
Retirement Gap Calculator

If your monthly burn rate is higher than your guaranteed income, multiply the gap by twelve to see the annual shortfall. Then consider how many years your retirement savings would need to cover that annual gap. Divide your total retirement savings by the annual shortfall. The result is the approximate number of years your current savings could sustain that gap without adjustment.

This calculation is not meant to discourage you. It is meant to show you why structure matters. If the number of sustainable years is lower than your expected lifespan, you now understand why action is necessary.

Housing Decision Matrix

Housing is often your largest lever. Ask yourself the following questions and answer them honestly.
Is my current housing cost aligned with my projected retirement income?

Could downsizing reduce my monthly expenses significantly?
Would relocating to a lower-cost region improve my financial stability?

Do I have equity that could be repositioned more strategically?
Would renting out a portion of my home create reliable supplemental income?

Write your answers in detail. Do not rush this section. Housing decisions often create the largest shifts in retirement math.
Income Skills Inventory

List every skill, certification, experience area, or specialized knowledge you possess. Include both professional and informal skills. Consider management experience, technical ability, teaching capacity, consulting potential, creative skills, and relationship networks.

Now ask yourself which of these skills could generate structured income without extreme physical strain. Identify at least two possibilities. Outline what it would take to begin monetizing them within the next ninety days.

Health Risk Awareness Checklist

Your health is a financial asset. Write down any current medical conditions that may affect your ability to work long term. Consider your family health history. Ask yourself whether you are investing time and attention into preventive care, exercise, nutrition, and stress management.

If a health event occurred within the next five years, how would it affect your income? Do you have sufficient emergency reserves? This exercise is not meant to create fear. It is meant to reinforce the connection between health and stability.

Social Security Timing Worksheet

Look up your projected Social Security benefit at different claiming ages. Compare the monthly amount at your earliest eligibility age, your full retirement age, and age seventy. Write each number down clearly.

Now calculate how delaying benefits would change your monthly gap. Would delaying allow you to increase lifetime income significantly?

Could structured part-time income allow you to wait longer and receive a higher monthly benefit? Write your conclusion.

Can I Relocate? Assessment

List the primary reasons you remain in your current location. Now evaluate whether those reasons are emotional, practical, financial, or habit-based. Research at least two lower-cost regions where your housing and living expenses would decrease meaningfully. Compare estimated monthly budgets between your current location and those alternatives.

Relocation is not mandatory. It is a lever. The purpose of this exercise is to determine whether it is a viable option for your situation.

Five-Year Stability Projection

Based on your answers above, outline a realistic five-year plan. Include projected reductions in expenses, anticipated supplemental income, planned debt elimination, and expected benefit timing. Write a brief narrative describing what your financial structure could look like five years from now if you follow your plan consistently.

This is not a fantasy exercise. It is a controlled projection based on deliberate action.

Closing Reflection

Write a final paragraph summarizing what you have learned about your current stability. Identify the single most important change you must make within the next twelve months. Commit to a start date.

Stability is not built through intention alone. It is built through measured action.

AFTERWORD

A FINAL WORD ABOUT TIME

Time feels different in your late fifties and early sixties than it did at thirty-five. The future no longer feels endless. Decisions feel heavier. Financial gaps feel more visible. The temptation in this stage of life is to look backward and measure what should have been done differently. But backward measurement does not create forward stability.

You are not the only one navigating this reality. Millions of capable, responsible adults reach this stage and realize their financial structure is thinner than they assumed. That realization does not mean you failed. It means the assumptions you were operating under no longer match the economic world you are living in.

The purpose of this book was not to alarm you. It was to clarify your position and restore leverage. Stability is rarely built in a single dramatic moment. It is built through measured decisions repeated consistently. Income repositioned. Expenses aligned. Benefits timed intentionally. Health preserved. Housing leveraged wisely. One structured year can redirect a trajectory that felt uncertain.

It is almost never too late to reduce risk. It is almost never too late to improve stability. It is almost never too late to change direction. What narrows over time is not possibility, but flexibility. And flexibility expands again when decisions become deliberate.

Retirement does not have to mean withdrawal from usefulness. It does not have to mean quiet anxiety about money. It can mean controlled pace, intentional income, reduced pressure, and thoughtful design. That version of later life does not arrive automatically. It is constructed.

You cannot control the years that have already passed. You can control how you use the years ahead. The difference between panic and stability is rarely luck. It is structure.

You still have structure to build. And that is enough.

ABOUT THE AUTHOR

Noah Wayan writes about the realities most people experience but rarely discuss openly. His work centers on growth, responsibility, aging, and the practical decisions that determine long-term stability.

In *The No Money Nightmare,* he speaks to the millions of adults who find themselves approaching retirement without the financial structure they once assumed would be there. With calm clarity and strategic insight, Noah offers readers not judgment, but direction — not hype, but structure.

He believes it is almost never too late to reduce risk, regain control, and build a more stable future - if one is willing to confront reality honestly and move with intention.

Noah's work is grounded in the conviction that stability is built deliberately, and that dignity can be preserved even during financial correction.

ALSO BY NOAH WAYAN

All Was Good Until You...is a powerful, eye-opening exploration of how emotional immaturity - hidden behind silence, control, and unhealed wounds - quietly erodes our closest relationships across every corner of life.

Can You Hear Me?...is a heartfelt call from men who feel invisible, ignored, or emotionally unheard. Through raw stories and powerful reflections, this book reminds us that being truly seen and understood can change everything.

Every Moment Counts...invites you to pause, reflect, and realign with what's truly important. Through soulful insights and gentle truth-telling, this book helps you step out of survival mode and into a life of intention, presence, and purpose.

I'm Ready Too!...This powerful guide shines a light on the emotional struggles men face when taught to hide their feelings. Through raw honesty and healing insights, *I'm Ready Too!* helps men break free from emotional silence, reconnect with their truth, and build deeper, healthier relationships. A must-read for any man ready to grow - and for those who love him.

The Do Book...s your wake-up call, your battle cry, your no-excuses guide to finally starting what you've been putting off. Whether it's launching that business, writing that book, going to the gym, or just making a move on a long-delayed dream - this short, sharp, and soul-stirring read will help you stop waiting and start doing.

From the Mind to the Hand...s your wake-up call, your battle cry, your no-excuses guide to finally starting what you've been putting off. Whether it's launching that business, writing that book, going to the gym, or just making a move on a long-delayed dream - this short, sharp, and soul-stirring read will help you stop waiting and start doing.

In **No Help Like Self Help** : Change Your Mind, Change Your Path, Noah takes you through his own journey of chasing success while battling obstacles like comparison, fear, and the infamous "Age Game." Through raw stories and powerful reflections, he reveals how he learned to replace poor thoughts with rich ones, give up on giving up, and step into the freedom of being his best self.

TA4UPublications.com

Made in the USA
Monee, IL
04 November 2026

67381919R00046